STRATEGIC IMPLICATIONS OF CHINA'S RISE ON U.S.–JAPAN RELATIONS

According to the 2010 National Security Strategy, our national security depends upon our military might, economic competitiveness, moral leadership, global engagement, and ability to shape an international system that serves the mutual interests of nations and peoples.[1] The 2010 National Security Strategy reaffirms U.S. strategic alliances and commitment to key nation-states within the Asia-Pacific region:

> Our alliances with Japan, South Korea, Australia, the Philippines, and Thailand are the bedrock of security in Asia and a foundation of prosperity in the Asia-Pacific region. We will continue to deepen and update these alliances to reflect the dynamism of the region and strategic trends of the 21st century.[2]

In view of the instability of the U.S. economy, the implications of which extend well beyond its borders, bilateral and multilateral agreements between allies have never been more critical. Indeed, given the volatile state of most economies, economic survival could overshadow other elements of national security. Competition for resources is forcing hard decisions and causing the United States to demand greater cost sharing among partners within the Asia-Pacific region. Complicated and stifling economic challenges are now forcing a 21st-century review of the U.S.-Japan Security alliance to keep it legitimate and current. The specific details of precisely how the agreement should or can be implemented is worthy of discussion. For generations, there has been no desire by Japanese political leadership, nor has there been a compelling reason for the United States, to encourage organic military capability beyond Japan's self-defense capability. Uniquely effective for over 50 years, the U.S.-Japan bilateral security alliance is still necessary. Historically, the Cold War between the United States and the Soviet Union, and an inwardly focused China, have allowed

Japan to take a minimalist approach to its self-defense environment. Unfortunately, the somewhat benign and tolerant environment that allowed for this moderate investment in military capabilities has rapidly changed in recent years. The current global economic climate and military growth of China necessitate a review of U.S. policy and defense strategy to support expansion in Japanese military capability to address 21st century regional threats.

<u>Why Change is Necessary</u>

Recent G20 reports cite an unprecedented undercurrent of global market isolationism. For instance, the U.S. has been unable to arrive at an agreement with South Korea to allow American beef, automobiles and automotive parts to more broadly penetrate its markets.[3] Not since the Great Depression has the United States experienced such global pressure to correct its financial situation, which has eroded since the late 1990s which exacerbates isolationist tendencies. As the United States continues to increase its exports, it is encountering more and more protective measures from importing countries. Isolationist behavior suppresses global economic growth, limits opportunities, and is counter a desired open and prosperous international economic system.

America's economic challenges also threaten national security. Policy-makers and economists need look no further than 2010 U.S. budget deficit to ascertain why equitable distribution of regional security costs and responsibilities have become so important. The U.S. national debt is approaching the $14.3[4] trillion spending cap set by law and little spending relief in sight while the U.S. remains engaged in operations in Iraq and Afghanistan. Future projections estimate that the budget deficit will grow by approximately $1 trillion per year over the next two years.[5] These conditions make it imperative to consider changes to achieving regional security with allied partners. Over 75% of the increase in the budget deficit since 2001 has accumulated from deliberate decisions, rather than factors outside of administration and lawmakers' control.[6] Tax cuts, military spending and rising health care costs account for the majority of the debt/deficit accumulation. It is debatable as to whether tax cuts sustained over the past decade should continue; what is not debatable is the decision itself—clearly the decision is within administrative and lawmakers' ability to control. Growing budgetary pressure caused by the continued support of unsustainable financial policy is a threat to U.S. National Security and the security of our allies. As a nation, the United States cannot continue to shoulder the Asia-Pacific security burden. Japan, South Korea and other regional partners must step forward and share a larger burden in addressing future threats to security.

China continues to emerge as a global super power, though there is considerable uncertainty regarding its intentions to compete peacefully. Recent Chinese actions with rare earth metals and natural resources in the African and South American continents suggest future competition for resources will be fierce. Maritime claims (global commons) and sea-lane access disputes also continue to generate friction between China and Japan. North Korea continues to contribute unpredictably to regional tension through disputes, altercations, and destabilizing incursions along the demilitarized zone with South Korea. These situations and others warrant continued vigilance and refinement of the U.S.-Japan Security Agreement to preserve future Asia-Pacific security and stability.

China's added pressure as a rising world power accentuates the need for U.S. fiscal reform. Today, China holds over $1.3 trillion (roughly 26%) of publically held foreign U.S. debt (with Japan and Great Britain following closely behind, with just under $1 trillion respectively).[7] China's U.S. debt holdings, growing economic strength and influence, and its ongoing investment in military growth pose the greatest potential threat to stability in the Asia-Pacific region. Liquidation of U.S. debt by China could be catastrophic to the United States.

U.S. -Japan Security Alliance

Since 1947, the U.S.-Japan Treaty of Mutual Cooperation and Security has contributed to regional security. Chapter II, Article 9 of Japan's Constitution stipulates that "aspiring sincerely to an international peace based on justice and order, the Japanese people forever renounce war as a sovereign right and the threat or use of force as means of settling international disputes."[8] Japan's current national defense policy incorporates the 1960 Treaty of Mutual Cooperation and Security with the United States, under which Japan assumes unilateral responsibility for its own internal security and the United States agrees to defend Japan against an external aggressor attack.[9] The Japanese Constitution authorizes self-defense as a responsibility of its government. Likewise, U.S. commitment to Japanese and Asia-Pacific stability and security is also specified in the U.S. National Security Strategy: "in partnership with our allies, the United States is helping to offer a future of security and integration to all Asian nations and to uphold and extend fundamental rights and dignity to all of its people."[10] Accordingly, U.S. alliances have preserved hard-earned peace and strengthened relations across the Pacific region in the second half of the 20th century.

The U.S.-Japan Treaty of Mutual Cooperation and Security has served both nations well for more than 60 years. To remain credible contributors to security and stability, it is essential that the U.S. and Asian partners maintain dynamic and adaptable security relationships in the 21st century.[11] For example, a willingness to allow China to shape events regionally, may address the immediate North Korean threat, while also promoting less reliance on U.S. influence in the region.

In a November 2010 Washington, DC address, Japanese Ambassador Ichiro Fujsaki articulated three defense options: first, increase defense spending and deterrence capability; second, depend on the goodwill of neighbors; and third, continue the security alliance with the United States.[12] His statements reveal a commitment to the continued pursuit of a strong alliance with the U.S. and increased investment in Japanese defense capabilities and specific technologies, such as missile defense.

Given the economic challenges facing the United States, Japan's most desirable course of action would be continued pursuit of all three areas outlined by the Ambassador (the options are not mutually exclusive and instead should be viewed as complementary). Continued reliance on the goodwill among neighbors strengthened by a regional bloc of partners could provide appropriate deterrence to a threatening North Korea and a rising China. It could also serve as an adaptable conduit for U.S.-Japan alliance coordination even further strengthening the formal agreement of U.S.-Japan Treaty of Mutual Cooperation and Security.

Establishing a new framework for ensuring Japanese and regional security should also dissuade Japan from independently deciding to develop nuclear weapons. Japan has long stood as a passionate advocate for nuclear non-proliferation. As the only nation to suffer a nuclear attack, it stands firmly behind its constitutionally mandated defensive posture. It also is firmly reliant upon the United States for offensive protection, if attacked. Nonetheless, it is believed that Japan possesses the technological capability to develop nuclear weapons for defensive purposes should the United States become unwilling or unable to protect Japan.[13] It remains in the interest of the United States that Japan does not pursue development of nuclear weapons. Such a decision would likely promote a nuclear arms race in the region, creating significant instability and the potential for catastrophic consequences in any conflict.

Evolving Asia-Pacific Policy and Strategy

The global financial crisis is prompting a holistic review of the ends, ways and means of U.S. National Security Strategy in Asia-Pacific. The United States remains committed to the goal of assuring Asia-Pacific stability through innovative, relevant and burden-sharing cooperative ways. As specifically outlined in the National Security Strategy 2010, "our alliances with Japan, South Korea, Australia, the Philippines, and Thailand are the bedrock of security in Asia and a foundation of prosperity in the Asia-Pacific region--We will continue to deepen and update these alliances to reflect the dynamism of the region and strategic trends of the 21st century."[14] As China's and India's global wealth and regional power increase, policy, strategy and focus will shift global attention and priority from the Middle East to the Asia-Pacific region.

As the third largest economy in the world, Japan is more than capable of shouldering more regional and global leadership and security responsibility. In the aftermath of 9/11, Japan passed groundbreaking anti-terrorism legislation allowing maritime self-defense forces (SDF) to deploy outside of the Asia-Pacific region. This further indicates Japan's adaptability and willingness to adjust constitutional interpretation to protect Japanese national interests.[15] Under the new anti-terrorism law, Japan has deployed forces to Iraq, has supported piracy interdiction operations off the coast of Somalia, and has conducted refueling operations in the Indian Ocean.[16] For example, Japan's contributions to Operation ENDURING FREEDOM (OEF) and Operation IRAQI FREEDOM (OIF) have included refueling support that dates back to 2001 and Japanese Self-Defense Force (JSDF) ground forces deployed.[17] Recent support has also included deployment of medical officers and nurses to Afghanistan.[18]

Clearly, Japan is leaning forward and taking on more security responsibilities. Japanese security transformation is also reflective of, and must remain adaptive to, a changing Asia-Pacific region. With the United States committed in Iraq through 2011, and in Afghanistan through 2014, even more Japanese military investment and self-reliance may be required. To protect its national interests into the future, Japan must be willing to accept these increased responsibilities.

U.S. Forward Deployed Presence Transformation

The changing forward presence of U.S. forces in the Pacific demonstrates commitment to regional allies and partners, and serves as a visible deterrent to potential aggressors, such as North Korea. This strategic posture has served U.S. interests for decades, but the landscape in the Western Pacific is changing. As technology advances and globalization continues to change the world, it is easy to question whether the U.S. can continue to pay the price required to keep robust presence at so many locations throughout the world. Other factors will also influence the future disposition of U.S. forces.

For instance, the presence of U.S. Marine Corps forces in Okinawa is an issue is worthy of mention. The negotiations to reconcile the relocation of Futenma airfield have tested both nations for over a decade.[19] For the past five years, the United States has remained firmly committed to keeping forces in Okinawa and continues to work with the Government of Japan and the local officials to find an alternate solution for basing. The firing of Party leader Mizuho Fukushima by Prime Minister Yukio Hatoyama's Cabinet is a reminder that irreconcilable government differences remain over the U.S. base and the congestion it causes on the southern part of Okinawa. Even though campaign promises to move Futenma helped the Democratic Party of Japan (DPJ) candidate win election, Prime Minister Hatoyama's position on the issue shifted towards preservation of the U.S.-Japan Mutual Cooperation and Security Agreement.[20] Continuing with what appeared to be an evident departure from Japan's Article 9 'no-war' clause to a more dynamic defense approach, the people elected the second DPJ Prime Minister, Naoto Kan in June of 2010.[21] Prime Minister Kan and current DPJ representation appear to be more agreeable to increased SDF military capabilities.

For the United States, Okinawa remains a strategic basing location, which serves not only as forward deployed presence for stability, but as a staging area capable of delivering significant combat power in the defense of U.S. interests should the need arise. On January 11, 2011, a new special measures agreement on facilities and area and the status of U.S. forces in Japan was reached. This agreement extended current Japanese cost-sharing levels through 2015[22] and affirmed agreements to relocate Futenma. These agreements remain contingent upon United States Government efforts to relocate 8,000 Marines to Guam, and to relocate and consolidate some 10,000 remaining Marines to bases in the northern Okinawa.[23]

The U.S. decision to move forces to Guam will help ease the tensions between the U.S. government and the local population on Okinawa. However, this move does not completely address the overall basing issue. It only begins to touch upon a problem created by Japan's decision to concentrate over 75% of U.S. Forces in Japan on Okinawa.[24] The Okinawa issue illustrates how the post-Cold War generation in Japan has grown less tolerant to U.S. military presence for deterrence and security purposes.

U.S. Navy Carrier Strike Group (CSG) and Amphibious Ready Group (ARG) homeports and force levels within the 7th Fleet Area of Responsibility (AOR) remain unchanged. The nuclear-powered USS *GEORGE WASHINGTON* and assigned CSG units remain home-ported out of Yokosuka, and the USS *ESSEX* and assigned ARG forces remain home ported out of Sasabo. Host nation relations remain supportive of current U.S. force levels. Both countries are addressing basing modernization issues to arrive at mutually acceptable solutions.

Strategic basing of U.S. forces on Guam is a clear future objective. In addition to movement of forces from Okinawa as mentioned previously, U.S. Air Force fighter/bomber utilization of Anderson Air Force Base (AFB) Guam increased significantly following the activation of a new Expeditionary Wing headquarters in 2003.[25] An increase in U.S. Navy attack submarines based on Guam occurred as recent as March 2011.[26]

China's Influence on U.S.–Japan Security Agreement

If history is our guide, it is understandable why tensions remain high between regional neighbors. China and Japan's adversarial history dates back centuries. Ninetieth and twentieth century conflict included two Sino-Japanese wars primarily motivated by an emerging and industrializing Japan and its imperialistic quest to gain land and access to resources to increase its security. Japan acquired an annexed and pro-Japanese Korean peninsula, and continued its imperialistic quest to secure resources in the second Sino-Japanese war that led up to World War II.[27] Ironically, the U.S. found itself defending China prior to and during World War II (WWII); however, after the world emerged from WWII and the Cold War between the United States and Russia began, the U.S. assumed responsibility as the security guarantor for Japan and the Asia-Pacific region. For much of the period following WWII, China, remained isolated and focused internally. China's subsequent rise has quietly positioned it as an influential U.S. near-peer competitor with global influence.

Amid rising tensions, recent altercations have prompted the United States into action. In July 2010, China claimed "indisputable sovereignty" over the South China Sea (SCS), but it insisted that it would continue to allow freedom of navigation within a waterway that handles over 50% of all merchant shipping tonnage throughout the world.[28] China based its claim on 1930s-era territorial maps of the entire SCS as proof that it belonged to the PRC.[29] China's claim remains unrecognized and incidents between China and regional countries continue.

At an October 2010 meeting hosted by Vietnam in Hanoi, leaders from 18 countries gathered at a U.S.-led meeting to discuss settlement of disputed territorial waters between China and neighboring countries, notably Japan and Vietnam.[30] The United Nations Convention on the Laws of the Sea (UNCLOS) provides the legal framework for a peaceful resolution of disputes relating to maritime security cooperation.[31] The UNCLOS charter requires that all members of the United Nations resolve maritime disputes peacefully. Japan, China, and the United States are among

10

the 161 countries that have ratified UNCLOS. At the forefront of China's contested sovereignty dispute are fishing rights, ownership of remote islands, access to seabed's that are potentially rich in minerals, and freedom of international waterways.[32] This aggressive Chinese declaration of sovereignty accompanied by provocation and lack of transparency in its military build-up are causes for regional and global concern. Stability in the Asia-Pacific region is paramount to the United States and its allies, and it is a professed concern of China as well. However, China's actions indicate otherwise and regional states are taking note.

U.S.-China Relations

Based on past performance and unwillingness to change, the lack of strategic transparency surrounding China's military build-up will only foster by speculation and doubt. China does not publish anything comparable to the U.S. National Security Strategy. Comprehension of Beijing's intentions can only be gleaned from periodic 'Defense White Papers' and speeches where "upholding national security and unity" and "ensuring interests in national development"[33] are mentioned. China-U.S. military-to-military engagement, supported by diplomatic efforts, are key elements to continued stability in the Asia-Pacific region. Severed U.S.-China relations over Taiwan arms sales have only recently renewed. As China's anti-access, area-denial and power projection capability grows, other Asian countries and allies have sought to foster and strengthen ties with the United States. U.S. Pacific Commander Admiral Willard, in his February 2011 interview, stressed continued monitoring of Chinese activity with a watchful eye on People's Liberation Army Navy (PLAN) capabilities that focus on its anti-access or area-denial capabilities.[34] Understandably, as China's wealth grows, so will its desire to expand influence and secure future interests.

11

U.S.-Chinese relations are exacerbated by the $6.4 billion arms deal between the United States and Taiwan in early 2010.[35] Taiwan remains a supported ally of United States and remains strategically supported by the U.S. through arms sales and maintenance of Taiwanese capacity to remain independent.[36] China maintains a long-standing ownership of Taiwan since Taiwanese independence was gained during the first Sino-Japanese war. Strained by the arms deal, U.S. and China relations remained tense before U.S. Secretary of Defense Robert Gates visit to China and Chinese President Hu Jintao's visit to the United States in January 2011. Then China unveiled its J-20 stealth fighter while Secretary Gates visited military facilities and other historical landmarks throughout China.[37] Strategically, this unveiling can either be perceived as a show of force or as a disconnect between the Chinese Communist Party (CCP) and its People's Liberation Army (PLA). Neither case is a positive development.

Global economics, regional security, and human rights issues have been constant topics in U.S.-China dialog. Over the past twelve months, China has outwardly expressed declaration of sovereignty through information and actions. China has confidently increased its global influence based on its economic success as most other nations deal with challenges. China has virtually unlimited ability to support its military modernization. Of greatest concern are its efforts to develop anti-ship ballistic missiles (ASBM). China's development of such a weapon significantly raises the potential threat to U.S. aircraft carriers and other military vessels transiting the SCS, and significantly the risks associated with any U.S. decision to defend Taiwan from Chinese attack.[38] ASBM capability also threatens U.S. Navy's dominance and credibility throughout China's near seas. Other emerging PLA capabilities that pose an increasing threat to

U.S. military power are space and cyberspace, joint interoperability, and civil-military integration of its homeland industrial complex.[39]

Economic Pressures

For two decades, China's economic success has financed sustained levels of investment in its military—military budgets remained at approximately 11% of Gross Domestic Product (GDP), supplemented by an additional 7.5% increase on March 4, 2010.[40] Supported by economic success, military investments for 2011 and beyond are expected to continue. In contrast, as the U.S. Department of Defense (DoD) awaits approval of a 2012 budget, most if not all branches are bracing for potentially dramatic cuts. In an effort to posture the military for inevitable spending cuts, Secretary Gates tasked the services in 2010 to identify $100 billion in savings.[41] Some believe that Gates' efforts were preemptive, designed to avoid Congressional mandates for even greater budget reductions. However, as proposals emerge from Congress to control the deficit, deeper cuts—beyond the $100 billion—appear likely.[42]

Budget deficits and compelling public desire to reduce spending have positioned the United States on a volatile and unstable fiscal path. President Obama recently received a clear message that the U.S. deficit has drawn worldwide concern, including that of Asia-Pacific allies. Two wars, multiple fiscal blunders, mismanagement by fiscal institutions, and natural disasters have mortgaged the U.S. to a tipping point. The U.S. now finds itself contemplating more isolationism at the same time increased engagement with global partners to share leadership and security responsibilities is paramount. Regardless of the path chosen, the U.S. must commit itself to more equitable burden-sharing relationships to preserve national interests, maintain legitimacy in the Asia-Pacific region, and further strengthen alliances with regional partners. In short, U.S. allies will need to assume additional financial responsibility for future security in the region.

Threats

Ballistic missile development remains a security threat to the United States and its allies, as do non-traditional threats such as natural disasters, terrorism, and proliferation of weapons of mass destruction. Advances in technology by potential adversaries (in terms of the capability to develop and the quality of ballistic missiles) threaten to outpace our defense capabilities. Combined defensive measures among regional partners, as well as continued efforts to reduce the proliferation of weapons of mass destruction and ballistic missile technology remain vital to stability throughout the region and the world. Regional actors such as Iran and North Korea continue to pursue long-range capabilities to reach and threaten the United States and its allies. Correspondingly, short-range ballistic missiles (SRBM), medium-range ballistic missiles (MRBM), and intermediate-range ballistic missiles (IRBMs) are growing at a rapid pace throughout the world.[43] Ballistic missile technology proliferation prevention and defensive measures must continue to advance at a pace that exceeds adversary pursuit or capability development.

Cost-sharing among regional partnerships in Europe, the Middle East, and East Asia are critical to sustaining research and development and fielding BMD capabilities as they develop and mature. Current systems such as PATRIOT batteries, the AN/TPY-2 X-Band radar, Terminal High Altitude Area Defense (THAAD) batteries, space-based sensors, and sea-based Aegis capabilities come at considerable cost. But these systems play a critical role in the mutual defense of allies and forward-deployed forces. Regardless of the source of the threat, missile defense remains a key issue in the U.S.

relationship with Japan. Japan's constitution clearly distinguishes self-defense, however, Japan has not constitutional obligation to intercept missiles launched over Japanese airspace destined for the United States.[44] As technology increases and Japan develops space and missile capabilities that extend beyond self-defense, this constitutional constraint arguably should be resolved.

Geostrategic Environmental Factors

The concept behind Sir Halford Mackinder's 'geopolitical pivot area' has helped shape policy and grand strategy for over a century. Mackinder's 'pivot area,' more commonly known as the 'Heartland' theory, posits that "he who controls the heartland, controls the World Island (Eurasia and Africa); he who controls the World Island, controls the World."[45] This strategic maxim remains relevant in today's environment. Alfred Thayer Mahan discussed the importance of the global commons and the capacity of sea power to facilitate peaceful trade. Clausewitz wrote that war is a continuation of policy through other means. He contended that war is simple, and that the simplest things can be the most difficult to achieve, especially if the relationship between ends and means becomes obscured by a failure to reach political objectives. Policy frames the overall strategic objectives specific to states and non-state threats. Opening the aperture and focusing on larger territories or regions to inform policy creates a desired geostrategic perspective and focus.

The 'Tyranny of Distance' between the United States and allies in the Asia-Pacific region is in fact sufficient reason to maintain a forward-deployed presence. Additionally, the Asia-Pacific region's geostrategic importance is resides in its contribution to free trade and access to global markets. To avoid future conflict in Asia-Pacific, regional partnerships and alliances with India, Indonesia, the Philippines,

15

Taiwan and other regional allies remains strategically critical to assure free trade and the flow of commerce. The Strait of Malacca is the 'Fulda Gap' of the twenty-first-century; it is where almost all shipping lanes between the Red Sea and the Sea of Japan converge, and where as much as 50% of all energy-related traffic will transit by the year 2020.[46] As the U.S. continues to reduce its presence in South Korea and Japan, it is vitally important that the U.S. maintain flexible strategic basing forward to sustain commerce flow through the Strait of Malacca and continue honoring security agreements with regional partners.

Design is an element of geostrategic environmental framing. In today's terms, design planning and environmental framing shape geopolitical policy. The U.S. Army defines environmental framing as a description of the current state of the operational environment and the desired conditions that constitute a desired end state. Design enables strategists to determine what is going on, what does it mean, why has the situation developed, and what is the real story by examining the tendencies and potentials of relevant actors and operational variables.[47] In review of history and in terms of what led to hostilities, U.S. policy of containment of communism dominated Cold War environmental framing of the Asia-Pacific region. Cold War geopolitical policy was framed by demonstrated Soviet Union hegemonic actions in Europe and feared expansion into Southeast Asia. The United States' Asia-Pacific geostrategic interest focused on continued access to resources, unrestricted passage through global commons and sea-lanes, regional stability and security responsibilities to allies, and containment of a perceived spread of communism by the Soviet Union and China.

These interests persist today. The new dynamic is an emerging China with undetermined aspirations and an unpredictable and potentially failing North Korea.

Cooperative Change Management

Japan's economic prosperity, the enormity of U.S. debt, and a world that has transformed to a multipolar environment are all factors, collectively viewed in context, that necessitate change to U.S. policy and defense strategy. As recently as October 2010, Japan announced the acquisition of six additional submarines to augment its fleet of 16; Japan announced these decisions amid concerns over rising tensions with China, whose submarine fleet had expanded to approximately 60.[48] There has never been a more urgent time for the United States and Japan to modernize their mutual defense agreement. Without question, both the U.S. and Japan have benefited from the current mutual security agreement. The end of the Cold War, threats to continued growth in globalization, increased trans-national threats, and proliferation advanced capabilities have increased regional tensions in the Asia-Pacific region.

While the United States historically invested wealth and capital to achieve military superiority, Japan limited its defense budget investments to less than one percent of its GDP.[49] Unavoidably, the current U.S. economic crisis means that U.S. allies must assume a greater share of costs of security. Cooperative bilateral and multilateral agreements with regional partners and allies can facilitate a more equitable distribution of leadership, resource expenditure, and overall security responsibility. In spite of this, a regional approach to security cannot and will not occur without open and honest debate.

Consequence Management

Holistically, China's rise to power and accompanying lack of transparency leave little room for miscalculation in the development and execution of an off-setting U.S.

policy and global strategy-and particularly Asia-Pacific strategy. Estimates indicate that China is at least ten to fifteen years behind the United States in technology and the capability to project power beyond its borders. But, without more transparency, these figures remain estimates. The U.S. must forge ahead with alliances and agreements to guarantee its security, the security of its allies, continued prosperity based on deterrence, balancing coalitions and alliances, and continued unhindered free trade.

In support of Japan's urgency to increase self-defense of its homeland and territories, Tokyo must come to grips with its constitution and aging cultural bias as a 'defensive state' that has forever renounced offensive capabilities. Due in large part to fiscal pressures that have mounted over the last decade, the United States will likely continue reducing forward presence globally with a goal of offsetting force level reductions with increased defensive capabilities.

An additional challenge to reduced presence at forward bases is deployment restrictions placed on U.S. forces by the host nations. The South Korean government has enforced political restrictions on U.S. military moves and has suggested that U.S. forces could not deploy without prior approval.[50] Japan has yet to impose the same restrictions; however, as tensions rise it is not beyond reason that Japan would attempt to exercise the same restrictions. Future basing of U.S. forward deployed forces should and should include flexibility to allow full utilization of all U.S. capabilities wherever and whenever required. Over the past three decades the strategic landscape of the world has transformed. The Asia-Pacific region has replaced the Atlantic as the engine of global trade and power following the collapse of Soviet Union and the subsequent rise of Japan, South Korea, and China, and an emerging India.[51] As the global strategic landscape has changed, so also must the U.S. role as the world's superpower likewise change.

Recommendations

The world becomes more volatile, uncertain, complex and ambiguous with each passing day. Without question, the current fiscal crisis that the United States is facing will necessitate cuts in the U.S. defense budget, as well as unprecedented fiscal cuts across the entire U.S. Government. Forward-based U.S. forces across the globe have been reduced dramatically over the past two decades and it is reasonable to expect that fiscal pressures will force the United States to remain focused on opportunities to reduce force levels even further. Aggressive defense-related research, development, and deployment of emerging capabilities must remain a priority for both United States and Japan, with both nations sharing the costs of meeting emerging regional threats.

Within U.S. Pacific Command, forward-based military personnel totals remain at approximately 325,000. Of that amount, Japan and South Korea host approximately 86,500 of this force. Japan has always been a generous host nation; it provides between $3 billion and $4 billion per year in host nation support (HSN).[52] On September 14, 2010, Japan also agreed to pay $498 million for facilities construction on Guam and to offset costs of moving Marines and their dependents from Okinawa to Guam.[53] This relationship is still a bargain for the United States. However, as budget savings are realized through force reductions and base consolidation, diplomatic initiatives must emphasize the reinvestment of savings in increased military defense capability. Without a better solution than relocating some U.S. forces from Okinawa to Guam, both nations should work forward an acceptable compromise to strengthen relations and achieve mutual defensive flexibility.

Japan and the United States should seize this opportunity and focus on the fundamental obstacle that is preventing the Japanese from further military build-up: its constitution. Specifically, language that addresses Japanese aspiration to forever renounce threat or use of force as a means of settling international disputes,[54] should be amended. Additionally, the Japanese and U.S. governments should continue to assess and identify opportunities for reprogramming host-nation support into more robust conventional capabilities that complement those already deployed in the region by the United States. Although Japan possesses the technological capacity to develop nuclear weapons, instead, Japan should invest in other capabilities.

Besides reducing the forward-deployed force, the United States should continue to invest in the infrastructure needed to optimize the strategic utility of Guam's location. By leveraging of Guam as a U.S. territory, the United States retains flexibility to deploy forces to any Asia-Pacific location without host-nation restrictions.

BMD, in terms of ways, offers a potential opportunity for the United States to reduce forward-deployed forces, strengthen cooperation with an allied partner, and an opportunity for Japan to enhance its security and self-sufficiency. In October 2010, the JS *KIRISHIMA* Aegis Cruiser, equipped with the U.S. Standard Missile 3 (SM-3) ballistic missile defense system upgrade, successfully located and destroyed a medium-range theater ballistic missile over the waters of Hawaii.[55] With four Japanese cruisers configured with the latest Aegis BMD system and more planned, Japan continues to enhance its naval missile defense capabilities. Additionally, Japan announced intentions in December 2010 to expand land-based U.S. Patriot PAC-3 systems to increase capability to defend against emerging North Korean ballistic missile threats.[56] Increased

BMD investment actions demonstrate cost sharing, leadership and self-sufficiency and are supportive of Japanese desires to maintain strong self-defense capabilities as U.S. economic recovery continues—these and similar BMD initiatives should be sustained. A better combined investment would be increased BMD capabilities to mutually protect regional allies or even the United States territories. As the Japanese constitution reads today, it is questionable, given future technological advancement in BMD, whether Japan would use that capability to defend another nation or ally.

Conclusion

Current Japanese constitutional language prevents the Japanese from pursuing military capabilities beyond what is required to provide defense of homeland and territories. In the event the U.S. becomes unwilling or unable to provide Japan with adequate security from emerging regional aggressors, this language should be amended. The Anti-Terrorism Special Measures Law passed by Japan's Diet following the 9/11attacks has nudged Japan's self-defense capability in a positive direction. However, Japan's constitution still stands in the way of true progress needed to forge a U.S.-Japan partnership that meets emerging 21st traditional and non-traditional threats to security. Since WWII, the United States has shouldered the burden of global leadership and has been the predominant provider of world stability and security. Terrorism, natural disasters, the global financial crises, two wars, and expanding domestic programs have all contributed in some way to the accumulation of unprecedented U.S. debt. As a nation, the U.S. risks losing the legitimacy of its global leadership role if economic difficulties continue or worsen. Smart decisions to change U.S. spending habits, better alignment of means to achieve strategic ends, and a more adaptable 21st-century regional security architecture could foster future tranquility, prosperity, and the continued blessings of liberty to the U.S. and the world. As the global environment changes, changes to U.S. policy and defense strategy must consider an adaptable approach to burden-sharing for regional security in the Asia Pacific region with Japan.

Endnotes

[1] Barack H. Obama, *National Security Strategy* (Washington, DC: The White House, May 2010), 7.

[2] Ibid., 42.

[3] Barry Gray, "G20 Summit Fails to Resolve Trade, Currency Conflicts," *Global Research CA*, November 14, 2010, http://www.globalresearch.ca/index.php?context=va&aid=21916, (accessed November 14, 2010).

[4] Andrew Taylor, "CBO: This Year's Budget Deficit to Hit $1.5T," *Associated Press*, January 26, 2011, http://news.yahoo.com/s/ap/20110126/ap_on_go_co/us_budget_deficit/print (accessed January 26, 2011).

[5] Ibid.

[6] Center on Budget and Policy Priorities, "Federal Budget Outlook," http://www.cbpp.org/slideshows/?fa=budget (accessed February 20, 2011).

[7] Steve Goldstein, "China's Treasury Holdings Revised by $268 bln," *The Wall Street Journal Market Watch*, February 28, 2011 http://www.marketwatch.com/story/chinas-treasury-holdings-revised-up-by-268-bln-2011-02-28?siteid=rss (accessed March 6, 2011).

[8] Constitution of Japan and Right of Self-Defense, Chapter 2 Article 9, http://www.mod.go.jp/e/d_act/d_policy/dp01.html (accessed 23 March 2011).

[9] Ibid.

[10] *National Security Strategy*, 42.

[11] Ambassador Ichiro Fujisaki, "A Changing Japan in a Changing World," *Brookings Institute,* July 8, 2010, http://www.brookings.edu/~/media/Files/events/2010/0708_fujisaki/20100708_Japan.pdf (accessed November 14, 2010), 30.

[12] Ibid., 4.

[13] Asia for Educators, "Article 9 and the U.S. – Japan Security Treaty;" *Columbia University*, http://afe.easia.columbia.edu/japan/japanworkbook/fpdefense/artnine.htm (accessed on March 6, 2010).

[14] *National Security Strategy,* 50.

[15] Hitoshi Tanaka, "The US-Japan Alliance: Beyond Futenma," *East Asia Forum,* February 16, 2010, http://www.eastasiaforum.org/2010/02/16/the-us-japan-alliance-beyond-futenma/ (accessed November 15, 2010).

[16] Ibid.

[17] Craig Martin, "The Case Against Revising Interpretations of the Japanese Constitution," *Asia-Pacific Journal: Japan Focus,* May 29, 2007, http://japanfocus.org/-Craig-Martin/2434 (accessed March 6, 2011).

[18] Rick Rozoff, "U.S. and NATO Drag Asia into Afgan Quagmire," *OpEd News.com,* October 29, 2010 http://www.opednews.com/articles/U-S-And-NATO-Drag-Asia-In-by-Rick-Rozoff-101029-690.html (accessed November 10, 2010).

[19] Tanaka.

[20] CNN Wire Staff, "Party Quits Coalition Government Over Okinawa Dispute," *CNN World,* May 30, 2010, http://articles.cnn.com/2010-05-30/world/japan.party.base_1_hatoyama-futenma-air-base-coalition-government?_s=PM:WORLD (accessed January 4, 2010).

[21] Martin Fackler, "Japan Elects a New Premier, Fifth in Four Years," *New York Times,* June 4, 2010, http://www.nytimes.com/2010/06/05/world/asia/05japan.html?_r=1 (accessed March 19, 2011).

[22] Agreement between Japan and the United States of America, *Special Measures Relating to Article XXIV of the Agreement Under Article VI of the Treaty of Mutual Cooperation and Security* (Tokyo, Japan), January 21, 2011 http://www.mofa.go.jp/region/n-america/us/security/agree0009.html (accessed on March 21, 2011).

[23] Bryan Wood, "U.S. Marine Corps Pacific Realignment Update," slides with scripted commentary, March 16, 2011, http://www.usmc.mil/unit/mciwest/WACO%20 Conference %202011/Wood%20-%20Guam%20Realignment.ppt (accessed March 19, 2010).

[24] Tanaka.

[25] Shirley A. Kan and Larry A. Niksch, "Guam: U.S. Defense Deployments," *Congressional Research Service Report for Congress,* January 7, 2010, http://www.fas.org/sgp/crs/row/RS22570.pdf (accessed March 23, 2011), 4-5.

[26] Corwin Colbert, "USS Oklahoma City Calls Guam Home," Commander U.S. 7th Fleet, March 5, 2011, http://www.c7f.navy.mil/news/2011/03-march/007.htm (accessed March 23, 2011).

[27] Herbert P Bix, "The Showa Emperor's 'Monologue' and the Problem of War Responsibility," *Journal of Japanese Studies* 18 (2) (1992): 295–363.

[28] John Pomfret, "Beijing Claims 'Indisputable Sovereignty' Over South China Sea," *Washington Post*, July 31, 2010, http://www.washingtonpost.com/wp-dyn/content/article/2010/07/30/AR201 0073005664.html?wprss=rss_world/asia (accessed December 28, 2010).

[29] Ibid.

[30] Craig Whitlock, "Gates Defends U.S. Role in Asian Sea Disputes," *Washington Post*, October 13, 2010, http://www.washingtonpost.com/wp-dyn/content/article/2010/10/12/AR2010101206316.html (accessed on December 28, 2010).

[31] *United Nations Convention on the Laws of the Sea*, United Nations Convention, (10 December 1982), 25.

[32] Whitlock.

[33] Office of the Secretary of Defense, *Military and Security Developments Involving the People's Republic of China 2010* (Washington DC: Office of the Secretary of Defense, August 2010), 13.

[34] Jim Garamone, "Willard Sites Need for Asia-Pacific Stability," *American Forces Press Service,* February 17, 2011 http://www.defense.gov/news/newsarticle.aspx?id=62859 (accessed on March 6, 2011).

[35] Whitlock.

[36] Legal Information Institute, "US Code Title 22, Chapter 48, Section 3301 – Taiwan Relations Act" http://www.law.cornell.edu/uscode/422/ usc_sec_22_00003301----000-.html (accessed on March 23, 2011).

[37] Elisabeth Bumiller and Michael Wines, "Test of Stealth Fighter Clouds Gates Visit to China," *New York Times*, January 11, 2011, http://www.nytimes.com/2011/01/12/world/asia/12fighter.html (accessed on March 19, 2011).

[38] Dean Cheng "The China Military Report and What's Left Unsaid," *The Heritage Foundation – Leadership for America*, August 23, 2010, http://report.heritage.org/wm2987 (accessed on December, 28 2010).

[39] Ibid.

[40] Office of the Secretary of Defense, 41.

[41] John T. Bennett, "Cuts Could Surpass Gates' Proposal," *Defense News*, November 15, 2010, http://ebird.osd.mil/cgi-bin/ebird/displaydata.pl?Requested=/ebfiles/e20101114788420.html (accessed on March 19, 2011).

[42] Ibid.

[43] Office of the Secretary of Defense, *Ballistic Missile Defense Review 2010* (Washington DC: Office of the Secretary of Defense, February 2010), iii.

[44] Masako Toki "Missile Defense in Japan," *Bulletin of the Atomic Scientists,* January 16 2009 http://www.thebulletin.org/ print/web-edition/features/missile-defense-japan (accessed on February 2, 2011).

[45] "Geopolitical Theory," A Geopolitical Guide to Japan, http://www.list.org/ ~mdoyle/jtheory.html (accessed on March 14, 2011).

[46] Robert D. Kaplan, *The Indian Ocean and the Future of the American Power* (New York, NY: Random House, 2010), Kindle e-book.

[47] U.S. Department of the Army, *The Operations Process,* Field Manual 5-0 (Washington, DC: U.S. Department of the Army, March 26, 2010), 3-5.

[48] Shared Comments, "Japan Adding Subs Amid Tension with China," *CNN*, October 21, 2010, http://news.blogs.cnn.com/2010/10/21/japan-adding-subs-amid-tension-with-china/ (accessed on November 14, 2010).

[49] Tanaka.

[50] Richard Halloran, "The Tyranny of Distance in the Pacific Command," *RealClearPolitics,* March 10, 2006, http://www.realclearpolitics.com/Commentary/com-3_10_06_RH.html (assessed on March 14, 2011).

[51] Ashley J Tellis, Andrew Marble, and Travis Tanner, *Asia's Rising Power and America's Continued Purpose* (Washington, DC: The National Bureau of Asian Research 2010-11), x.

[52] George R. Packard, "The United States-Japan Security Treaty at 50 Still a Grand Bargin?" *Foreign Affairs* 89, no.2 (March/April 2010).

[53] Travis J. Tritten, "Japan Agrees to Pay $498 Million Toward Guam Buildup," *Stars and Stripes*, September 14, 2010, http://www.stripes.com/news/pacific/guam/japan-agrees-to-pay-498-million-toward-guam-buildup-1.118239 (accessed on March 23, 2011).

[54] Constitution of Japan and Right of Self-Defense.

[55] Jim Wolf, "U.S. and Japan Stage Successful Missile-Defense Test," *Reuters,* October 29, 2010, http://www.reuters.com/assets/print?aid=USTRE69S0S120101029 (accessed on March 6, 2011).

[56] United Press International, "Japan Will Strengthen Missile Defense," *UPI.com*, December 11, 2010, http://www.upi.com/Top_News/World-News/2010/12/11/Japan-will-strengthen-missile-def (accessed on March 6, 2011).

www.ingramcontent.com/pod-product-compliance
Lightning Source LLC
Chambersburg PA
CBHW080808290526
45790CB00008B/3613